W9-BRH-458

To:

_____

From:

_____

Date:

_____

Put a Little "Happy" in Your Life

Photography by **Christina Bynum Breaux**

HARVEST HOUSE PUBLISHERS
EUGENE, OREGON

*I dedicate this book to my wonderful husband
who has so generously opened his home
and his heart to all the children that God has
brought to our doorstep.*

A portion of the artist's proceeds of this book goes to Stepping Stones Foundation. Stepping Stones Foundation makes mentoring their mission by providing year-round support to local area children in need of clothing, food, and shelter. www.steppingstonesfoundation.net

Put a Little "Happy" in Your Life

Text copyright © 2013 by Harvest House Publishers. Original text by Jeff Marion.

Published by Harvest House Publishers
Eugene, Oregon 97402
www.harvesthousepublishers.com

ISBN 978-0-7369-4960-6

Design and production by Katie Brady Design and Illustration, Eugene, Oregon

Printed in China

13 14 15 16 17 18 19 / FC / 10 9 8 7 6 5 4 3 2 1

Raise your hand if you want more
"**happy**" in your life.

If you're ready to **soar**

or dive in **deeper**,

then maybe it's time
to come out of your cocoon

and **launch** yourself headfirst into life!

You might need to **shape up** a little bit

or develop an interest in higher *learning,*

but the happiness is oh so *sweet*

when you finally reach your goal.

Have you ever **stopped** to consider
what life might be like

if you trusted **God** and just went for it?

Maybe it's time to take that
dream *vacation*

or take up a **musical** instrument.

Perhaps a brand-new *hairdo*

or a cool new *outfit* would do the trick.

Don't sit around **waiting** for something to happen.

Just do whatever it takes to get your motor **running!**

So what if some of your friends think
you're going **crazy?**

You can always make new friends who
are just as **crazy** as you are.

After all, you always have the
support of your family

and others who **care** in life's
little emergencies.

Just keep on being **you**

and never ever **sell** out!

With God's help, you can have
a *beautiful* life.

Hang on to these few simple *truths*...

When life gets too **hot** to handle,

chill out.

Laugh harder than ever before

and *love* more sincerely.

God wants you to reach out to those
who are **different** than you are,

but remember your
old friends need you too.

Always keep a *stiff* upper lip

because you have no idea what God
might put in your path.

Celebrate this life He gave
you to the fullest

but stay focused and maintain your **balance.**

Make sure you have the right gear
to get the job done

or learn to **accept** the consequences.

God will help you take that next big step

and give you the courage to stand up
for what's important.

The waters might seem **calm** right now,

but trust me, life can get **rough** in a hurry.

There will be days when the *pieces*
just don't match up,

and it seems like no one is buying
what you're selling.

It might feel like God is **stretching** you
beyond your limits

or putting the **squeeze** on you,

but you'll be *tickled* pink to discover

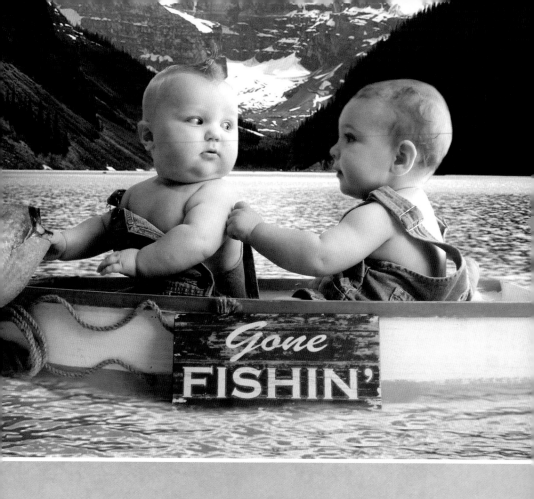

that everyone is in the same boat.

Even for a **king**

or a **queen**, life can be a
royal pain sometimes.

So instead of crossing over to the **dark** side,